A Letter from the King of Portugal

A PUBLICATION FROM THE

James Ford Bell Collection

IN THE UNIVERSITY OF MINNESOTA LIBRARY

Copy of a Letter of the
King of Portugal Sent to the King of Castile
Concerning the Voyage and Success of India

TRANSLATED BY

Sergio J. Pacifici

1955

THE UNIVERSITY OF MINNESOTA PRESS · MINNEAPOLIS

Introduction

W<small>HEN</small> Vasco da Gama returned to Lisbon from India on August 29, 1499, he brought a century of Portuguese exploration and reconaissance to its conclusion, and inaugurated a new era of commercial and colonial expansion in the East. After Portuguese navigators had made countless voyages along the west coast of Africa to seek the products of that continent, contact with the legendary Christian kingdom of Prester John, and an all-water route to India, da Gama finally proved that the much-wanted spices of India could be brought to Europe by a route around the Cape of Good Hope.

Manuel the Fortunate, king of Portugal, lost no time in attempting to exploit the newly found passage, and thereby make Portugal the link between the demand for spices in Europe and the supply in the East. On March 8, 1500, he sent a flotilla of thirteen ships to India, and in the four years following, three similar expeditions were undertaken.

The first of these fleets was commanded by Pedro Álvares Cabral, a member of one of Portugal's noble families. Cabral's expedition is historically important as the first major commercial voyage to India made by the Cape of Good Hope route, and on his outward voyage he touched the coast of Brazil, thereby establishing Portuguese commercial and colonial interest in two hemispheres. With this voyage and those immediately following, Portugal established herself as the dominant spice merchant of Europe, breaking the hold of the Egyptian and Italian merchants upon the Eastern trade.

On October 28, 1505, there appeared in Rome a news tract printed by John of Besicken which purported to be a "Copy of a letter of the King of Portugal sent to the King of Castile concerning the voyage and success of India." Although certain textual evidence tends to indicate that this was merely a news publication with a spectacular title, it is nevertheless significant, for it not only gives a contemporary account of these first four commercial ventures to India by the Portuguese, but it also contains the first printed reference to the discovery of Brazil. It is, therefore, a document of interest to the history of two continents as well as to the larger history of commerce.

The number of copies of this "letter" that were printed is not known, but only four copies of the first edition are recorded at present. They are located in the British Museum, the Marciana Library in Venice, the Corsini Library in Rome, and the James Ford Bell Collection at the University of Minnesota. Of the later 1505 Milan edition, the only copy known is also in the James Ford Bell Collection.

In undertaking to publish rare items relating to the early history of commerce, we have selected John of Besicken's news letter for its vivid description of the Portuguese spice trade, which was, in fact, the starting point for direct commerce between Europe and the East, and for its format which is typical of the early sources of popular information on the new discoveries in the early sixteenth century. While it has been reprinted in the Italian, and translated into Portuguese, this translation by Sergio J. Pacifici is the first English edition of this work.

John Parker

Curator, James Ford Bell Collection

UNIVERSITY OF MINNESOTA

Translator's Note

IN TRANSLATING this anonymous account of the early Portuguese voyages to India, I was confronted with two alternatives: either the translation was to be rendered exactly, and consequently preserve its original cumbersomeness, or it might be rendered into a flexible and grammatically correct English. The latter alternative was selected as it was believed that readability was to be the most important feature of this work.

In the interest of clarity, therefore, sentences have been broken up when necessary, conjunctions have been added or suppressed to insure continuity, and words have sometimes been interpolated. I should, therefore, like to view my work as an adaptation from the Italian original rather than a translation in the strict sense of the word.

Whenever possible, I have translated the names of persons and places appearing in the text, but have left terms describing currencies and measurements in the original.

The work of a translator is seldom a one-man task, and I should like to express my gratitude to my friend Dr. Rigo Mignani of the University of Washington for his able help in reading and interpreting obscure words and sentences. I am also deeply indebted to Professor Thomas G. Bergin of Yale University for reading my translation and for offering a number of improvements. As translator, I am, of course, fully responsible for whatever flaws still mar this version.

I have read with interest and profit William Brooks Greenlee's *The Voyage of Pedro Álvares Cabral* (translated with introduction and notes by William Brooks Greenlee, London, The Hakluyt Society, 1938). His translation of related documents and his background material have been especially helpful.

Sergio J. Pacifici

YALE UNIVERSITY
NEW HAVEN, CONNECTICUT

The next two pages are facsimile reproductions of the first and last pages of the original published version of the letter

ꟲ Copia de vna littera del Re de Portagallo mãd ata
al Re de Castella del viaggio e successo de India·

Ｂ Enche catholico Re e signore dapoi iltrafico e comer∕
tio in le parte de India a nome nro comiciato piu volte
del successo p altre mie·v·Serenissima maiestade habbia adul
sato:pur al psente pla venuta de certe nre naue me e parso cõ
deceuole dele loro noue far certa ꝗlla·Et replicãdo quãto ple
altre nre hauemo scritto:acio del tutto sia optimamẽte iforma
ta:redurli a memoria dala pma nra armata pinsino alla psente
ꝫurno le nre prime naue a ꝗlla parte mãdate·ꝛꝰ·de numero: prima armata
e vna garauella quale era carcha de victuarie· Queste de lo
anno·ＭＤ·a giorni octo de marzo se partirno del nro porto   Anno·ＭＤ·
de Lixbona p andare in mercãtia de speciarie e drogarie alle
parte de India vltra il Mare rosso e persico ad vna Citade
chiamata Calichut:ꝯl Re Sito:costumi e modi de epsi dir e
mo de sotto·De dicta armata fu Capitanio generale Petro   Capitanio ge
aluez Cabrale· Nauicando passato il capo verde scoperseno   nerale·
vna terra nouamẽte a notitia de ꝗsta nra europa venuta:alla
qule terra o Santa croce pose il neme: e ꝗsto pche nel litto   Terra dsanta
fece adrizare vna altissima croce:altri la chiamano terra nuo∕ croce·
ua ouero mũdo nuouo·E ꝗsta terra doue sorseno vltra il tro∕
pico ꝯl Cancro gradi·xiiij·como li marinari p li suoi quadrãti Sito de dicte
e astrolabij tolsino laltura pche cõ instrumẽti astrologici naui terra.
cano a ꝗlle parte· Partendosi dal dicto·C·verde e posta fra
ponẽte e le becchie venti pncipali distante dal dicto·C·verde
leghe·cccc· Deli habitatori:fertilitate:magnitudine:cõditiõe:
e se sia Insula o terra ferma p altre nre hauemo dato piena in
formatione a·v·S·Che li partendosi dicta armata lasso dui
christiani alla ventura:portaua vinti homini gia p iusticia con
dénati a morte p poterli lassare doue meglio al Capitanio pa
resse·De ꝗsti dui homini poi p vnaltra nra armata cõ directiua∕
mẽte mãdamo a ꝗlla terra: torno vno ilꝗle scia la loro lingua
e detene informatiõe del tutto·De ꝗsta terra il Capitanio ne
remando indricto quella garauella che portaua victuarie·
ꟲ Il secundo giorno del mese de Mayo fecero vela verso il   Capo o bona
capo de bona speraza e al·xij·giorno furno a vista ꝯl dicto C· speraza; terra
cõ e lontano da dicta terra·Mcc·leghe· Questo C·de bona   vltra lo equi∕
speraza e vltro lo equinoctiale p·xxxi·grado e e quella terra   noctiale·

a

℃ Et con questa armata sono venute oue altre naue Capita
nio dela vna e Ruilorenzo:delaltra Saldagna:quale gliatri
anni se partirno de qui per andare de armata in quelle parte:
τ per fortuna se transcorseno nel mare rosso : in certe insule
doue sono state·rvi,mesi; τ mai laltra nra armata ba babuto
de epse noticia·In questo tempo banno prese molti nanigli τ
abrusiati;τ facti molte correrie per terra: perche vna de dicte
naue e taffozea che porta·rr·canalli:τ ba la poppa aperta cõ

naue taffozea

vno ponte de·rrr·bracia quale gietra i terra:τ p epso saglino
τ intrano li canalli· In questo modo bãno facto grandissimo

Canibar·
Barbara·

danno:in tanto che vn Re de Canibar τ il Re de Barbara
grandi signori:p bauere pace gli donorno trenta mil·mitigali
de auro:vn mitigale vale vn ducato e mezo deli nostri:liquali

Mccccc v·
Naue·rrrvã
no in India·

ne banno portati;τ molte altre richeze· ℃ Nel anno presente
del mese de Marzo mãdassemo p le dicte parte·rrr·naue ben
armate alle qle babiamo imposto remandino qlle che sono la
de armata · Et che oue de epse passino ascopure L aprobani
insula:quale dicono essere li vicina·Quatro de dicte naue bã
no ãdare a Zaphala doue speramo bauere acordato il trafico
Aspectaremo quello seguira τ prepararemo alcuna naue per
lo anno sequéte·Dio conseru vostra Serenissima ma·longo
tempo in tranquillo stato : τ noi insieme con epsa acio possia
mo vedere questa nra nauicatione pacifica τ quieta ad laude
τ augmento de nostra sancta fede·

℃ Impresso in Roma per maestro Joanni de Besicken·
nelanno·Mccccc v·a di·rriij·de Octobre.

❡ Copy of a Letter of the King of Portugal Sent to the King of Castile Concerning the Voyage and Success of India

ALTHOUGH, my Catholic King and Lord, I have advised more than once Your Most Serene Majesty of our success in other letters of mine, after we had already begun our traffic and trade in the lands of India in our name, yet, at the present time, because of the arrival of some of our ships, it has seemed opportune to me to make a report of their news. And repeating whatever we have written in our previous letters, in order that you might be excellently informed of everything, it has seemed opportune to me to recall all the information from the time of our first armada right up to the present armada. The first ships we sent to those lands were twelve in number, plus a caravel full of *First Armada* provisions. These ships left our port of Lisbon in the year 1500, on the 8th day of March, to go and trade in spices and *1500* drugs in the lands of India, beyond the Red and the Persian Seas, to a city called Calicut. Of the King, site, customs, and manners of these lands we shall speak later on. Pedro Álvares Cabral was the Captain General of the afore-men- *Captain* tioned armada. Sailing past Cape Verde, they sighted a land *General* which had recently come to be known in our Europe, to which they gave the name of Santa Cruz, and this because *Land of Santa* they had a very high cross erected on its shore. Others call *Cruz* it New Land, that is, New World. This land, where they

3

came ashore, is situated on the 14th meridian beyond the Tropic of Cancer, as the sailors found its position by means of their quadrants and astrolabes, since they sail in those parts with astrological instruments. This land is situated 400 leagues west-southwest of the afore-mentioned Cape Verde. We have previously advised Your Lordship of its inhabitants, fertility, size, and condition and whether it is an island or a continent. The armada, upon its departure, left two Christians to chance. It was carrying 20 convicts, previously condemned to death, to be left wherever the Captain might deem fitting. Later on, one of these two Christians came back with another armada we had sent directly to that land. This man knew their language and gave information about everything. From there the Captain sent back the caravel carrying the provisions. On the 2nd of May they sailed toward the Cape of Good Hope and on the 12th they sighted that Cape, situated 1200 miles away.

This Cape of Good Hope is situated on the 31st meridian beyond the Equinox, and Ptolemy in his outline of Africa leaves it as unexplored land. The coast is inhabited by people not too black, and is fertile and abundant with every fruit and water. From the observations made by the sailors, its people have journeyed to the Antarctic Pole, and know Aquarius and most other constellations, of which they have the descriptions. While sailing toward Africa, for ten consecutive nights the sailors saw a very large comet. Also they saw the celestial arc right in the middle of the night—something unheard of amongst our people. On the 24th day of the same month, the weather being good, as they were sailing round the mentioned Cape Verde,* they suddenly met with a very strong wind which sank right there four of the ships together with all their crews. Two more got lost; the

---

* In his *Asia* (Lisbon, 1552, I, 56), João de Barros describes the storm as occurring in the South Atlantic between the landfall made in Brazil and the Cape of Good Hope.

4

rest, carried off by a following wind, with sails, rigging, rods, and masts torn, were left to chance for five days. Finally, once the sea had calmed down, the ships, which were six in number, came together. Sailing by the coast they passed Sofala. This is an island at the mouth of a river, and is inhabited by many merchants. There gold is abundant and is brought to them from the interior of Africa by men small in body, strong, and very ugly, and with small voices, who eat human flesh, mainly that of their enemies. This is the same manner in which gold is brought to our mine in Guinea. This island, too, belongs to the King of Quiloa. Past this island, they found two big ships coming from Sofala and going to the King. These two ships were held by our Captain, but once he understood that they belonged to the aforesaid King he let them go free, taking from them only a pilot to guide them to Quiloa. Arriving in Quiloa, principal city of this great and well-populated kingdom, with a safe-conduct, the Captain was much honored by that King because he was carrying our letters written in Arabic, and our directives to the King to grant him the traffic and trade of this island. And this was granted to him. But since two ships which were to remain there were being held, he did not demand any ransom. Quiloa is a city in Arabia, situated on a small island connected with the Continent, well populated by Negro merchants, and built in our ways. Here there is an abundance of gold, silver, amber, musk, and pearls, and the people wear silk and fine cotton clothes without excess. Leaving from there, they sailed towards the kingdom of Malindi, to the King of which they were similarly bringing my letters and message since he had graciously received don Vasco [da Gama], who was the first to discover this coast. There, in the harbor of Malindi, they found three ships of Cambay of 200 barrels each. They are ships built with canes above and wood shiplaps tied with

The island of Sofala

Two ships are captured

Malindi

5

ropes and pitch at the bottom, since they do not have nails. All the ships in those lands are of this kind. They always sail with wind astern because they cannot go into the wind; they have a quarter-deck. The King talked with our Captain through interpreters, and signed a pact of good friendship between us, giving the Captain a pilot to lead him to Calicut. There two other convicts remained, one of whom was to remain in Malindi, the other to seek refuge elsewhere on the land. These two kingdoms, Quiloa and Malindi, are on the west side of the Red Sea, adjacent to the territories of the Gentiles and Prester John, whom they call *Abechi* in their language—which means iron-branded, because in this fashion in fact they brand themselves with hot steel and thus they are baptized without water. The 7th day of August they left for Calicut and passed a gulf 700 leagues wide. They sighted Calicut the 12th of September, six months after their departure from Lisbon. One league from the harbor of Calicut, the citizens and gentlemen of the King came to greet them with great festivities. They docked before the city and fired the artillery, which caused great admiration among the inhabitants. Calicut is in India, and to it are brought spices and drugs; it is densely populated with Gentiles. For this reason, there are merchants of these goods from many lands and trades, like Bruges in Flanders or Venice in Italy. The following day the Captain sent to land four Indians whom he had brought from Lisbon, and who spoke Portuguese fluently. They received a safe-conduct from the King in order that our people might be allowed to land as the Captain had ordered. So Alfonso Furtado came ashore and he agreed with the King that five gentlemen should be sent to the ships as hostages, in order that the Captain might land safely and parley with him. The Captain landed, leaving in his place Sancho de Tovar in charge of the ships. The King, carried on a litter, came to the shores to receive the Captain, who was carried in the arms of the King's gentlemen right up to the King's presence. The King was lying down in a litter covered by a purple silk cloth. From his waist up he was naked, from the waist down he was clothed with a cloth of cotton, worked with gold and silver. He had on his head a cap of brocade made like an antique helmet. From his ears there hung two pearls, as big as hazelnuts, one round and the other pear-shaped. He wore two gold bracelets with many jewels and pearls and an infinite number of rings on his hands. All those gems were very precious and of great price. There was also a large chair made completely of silver. Its arm-rests and the back were of gold with many precious stones. There were 20 trumpets of silver and three of gold, a third longer than ours and quite loud. In the room there were six Moorish lamps of silver, which burned day and night. No one of the bystanders can approach the King nearer than six paces, out of reverence, but the Captain came closer than the others and, sitting down, relayed his message and gave the King our letters written both in Arabic and in our tongue. And at once the Captain sent for our presents, which were as follows: first, a basin and a large gilded silver jug, worked with many figures in relief; a large covered bowl and a large gold cup worked with figures; two silver maces with their own chains; four cushions, two of brocade and two of crimson velvet; a baldachin of brocade with gold and crimson fringes; a large carpet; two cloths of fine satin, one with foliage, the other with figures. The King graciously received these gifts because these things are un-usual in those lands, and concluded a pact of peace and friendship. As a token of this pact, the King ordered that a letter be written on a sheet of beaten silver with his seal made of damascened gold, according to their customs—a letter which has been brought to me, along with other let-

The Captain talks with the King

Friendship of the King

7

ters, written on leaves which seem to be those of a palm tree, on which they commonly write. Sugar, honey, oil, wine, water, vinegar, charcoal, and cordage for ships are made from these trees, and they constitute the chief provision to be carried at sea. Afterwards, the King dismissed the Captain, saying that he could go back to the ship and send back to the land the five hostages, who had not eaten while aboard the ship. These hostages, seeing the Captain return and fearing that they would be detained in custody, threw themselves into the water and some of them fled to land. Some of them were captured by the sailors, and the Captain insisted in not returning them until the King had sent back Alfonso Furtado with eight Christians, along with some goods which had remained on land. In this restitution there was a certain amount of discord, because one side did not trust the other. After this restitution, by the will of the King and the Captain, Ayres Correa landed. He was to remain there as our business agent. In exchange, two nephews of a merchant of Guzerat came aboard the ship. This agent, after being on land two and one-half months, with much labor succeeded in having the traffic granted, although many merchants—and chiefly those of Mecca— were against it. Following the agreement, the King consigned to our agent a large house overlooking the shore. The business agent took possession of the estate with our banner, and began dwelling in it. The two merchants who were aboard went back to the land; and then immediately the factor began loading our ships, since the King had promised him the cargo before anyone else. At the request of the King, the Captain, according to their agreement, sent a caravel with 70 men and a large bombard and other artillery to capture a large Moorish ship armed with 400 archers, and so captured it, presenting it afterwards to the King in his name. And to the King it seemed a great wonder

Discord

A caravel captures a Moorish ship

8

that it had been captured by such a little boat. There were on the afore-mentioned ship many goods and five elephants, extremely well trained in warfare, which were appraised at 30,000 ducats. On the 16th of December, while our factor was busy with the inventory of two ships being loaded, our Captain detained a Moorish ship which, heavily laden, wished to depart secretly as it had been agreed with the King. At once all the merchants took up arms and started a tumult in the city and ran to the house of our factor where there were about 80 Christians and, after a fight of three hours, demolished it completely, although in the meantime many Moors were killed. The factor, together with other people, once the house was lost, retreated to the sea where the barges of the ships had come, after having heard the noise. But a great multitude came up, and the factor and 53 Christians were killed. The others escaped, wounded. In the meantime the Captain was sick, and having heard the news, waited a day to see whether the King would make any amend for this incident. And seeing that the King was not concerned over it, he ordered that ten large ships that were there be captured and, having unloaded their cargoes, they found three elephants which they ate later on, because of a dearth of provisions. He slew the greatest part of the people, and the rest whom he made prisoner he ordered to be burned in sight of the city. The following night, he had all ships drawn near the land, and at dawn he began bombarding the city, which did not have any wall and which was greatly damaged, so much so that the King was forced to abandon his palaces. Afterwards, they sailed into a harbor of the afore-mentioned King, called Fundarane, killed many people with their artillery, and decided to go towards the Kingdom of Cochin, which is 40 leagues beyond Calicut. On the way, they found two ships of the King of Calicut which they took and burned. On the

Five elephants

Death of the Christians

They burn the Moors' ships

24th of December, they arrived at Cochin and were graciously received by that King. They made agreements with him and in 16 days they had the ships loaded, since spices and drugs go from these lands to Calicut. This King is so very powerful that two merchants had 50 of their own best ships fighting against the King of Calicut. And in exchange for seven of our men who were on land in order to trade, the King sent to the ship two of his gentlemen who, every time they wished to eat, had to land because if they eat while at sea, according to their laws, they are not allowed to go before their King. In this kingdom there are many Christians converted by St. Thomas, whose apostolic life their priests follow with great devotion and strictness. They have churches where there is only the cross and celebrate Mass with unleavened bread and wine, which is made from raisins and water as nothing else is available to them. All Christians go with their hair uncut and beards unshaved. From these people our men learned that the body of St. Thomas lies 150 leagues from Cochin, on the seacoast, in a city of small population called Mailapur. Our men have brought some earth from his tomb, which is visited by many Christians and by all those peoples because of many miracles. And they have also brought two Christian priests who, with permission from their superior, have come here to go to Rome and Jerusalem, since they believe that the Church of St. Peter is better governed than theirs. They also learned that beyond the aforesaid resting place of St. Thomas there are many Christian peoples who come on pilgrimages to the tomb of this saint. They are white men with fair hair and green eyes and are quite strong. They call their principal city Malchima, whence come large and beautiful vases of porcelain, musk, amber, and aloe wood, which they get from the Ganges River which is in their land. Once these ships were loaded, there appeared

Loading of our ships

Christians of St. Thomas

City of Mailapur

10

a fleet of the King of Calicut of 80 sail boats with 15,000 men, at the sight of which our Captain sailed away and, upon his departure, left 7 Christians in Cochin, taking along two gentlemen hostages; he intended, however, to return. But afterwards, seeing that the weather was good, he decided to return home, and thus the Moors and the two prelates are with us now. He also did not wish to clash with such an armada of Calicut, since he had his ships loaded and manned by few people, and also in view of the fact that the voyage was long and they were still 4000 leagues from Lisbon. Thus, during the voyage home, on the 15th day of January 1501, they passed by another kingdom, called Cananor, on the west side of Calicut. Its King sent a cargo to be offered to the Captain, wishing to extend credit until his return. But the Captain, thanking him, accepted only 100 chantaras of cinnamon, and immediately paid for them. The Moors brought the cinnamon to the ships with their boats and sent one of their gentlemen, who is now with us, with letters and messages. From this kingdom the hostages of Cochin wrote to their King and their relatives, and similarly our Captain wrote to our Christians who had remained there. The following day, the Captain sailed for Malindi and on the last day of January they found a large ship loaded with goods, which they allowed to proceed since it belonged to the King of Cambay, taking only a pilot from it to guide them to Malindi. At midnight of the 12th of February one of our ships of 200 tons ran aground. The crew was saved. The Captain of this ship was Sancho de Tovar. Thus there remained five ships, one of which our Captain sent back to Sofala to investigate conditions there. Later on, in a tempest, another ship was lost. Finally, however, on Palm Sunday the ships rounded the Cape of Good Hope and arrived at Beseguiche connected with Cape Verde; and there they calked some of their ships. Finally,

Departure of our armada

The city of Cananor

One of our ships lost

one of the ships which had gotten lost arrived together with the ship previously sent to Sofala. The Captain of the latter said that he had sent a Christian in exchange for the hostage of a Moor to Sofala and had waited three days. Not receiving any news from him, he had left, taking along the Moor who has given ample information about this land—as we have previously written above. Afterwards, they came _Arrival in Lisbon_ toward Lisbon and arrived on the 21st of July 1501, and brought spices and drugs of excellent quality for a good price. More recently, one of the ships of those that got lost rounding the Cape of Good Hope—where the four ships sank—has arrived. This ship fortunately ran into the Red Sea and, having lost its boats and the greater part of its crew, has miraculously returned with seven persons and has brought a good quantity of silver vases bought in those _Six ships return_ lands. So out of twelve ships which left for India, six have returned; the others have been lost. Your Most Serene Majesty will be able to learn in more detail about the size of those lands, the quality of their shores, the latitude and navigation course followed on this trip by the charts I am sending you. The same year, on the 10th of April, not receiving any news from the first armada I had sent to those parts, I _Four ships leave_ sent four other ships in good order. These ships, since they already had knowledge of that new land called Santa Cruz, went there to replenish themselves, because certainly this land is very necessary to a trip of this kind. From there they passed the Cape of Good Hope, and without finding any of our four ships, they went up to the coast of India without stopping. Before arriving at Calicut they found two Moorish ships loaded with spices and drugs which were going to Mecca. From these Moors, captured by force, they learned of the war and the discord that had occurred between our armada and the King of Calicut, since these ships were coming laden from that land. At once the

12

Captain of the aforesaid four ships, who was Gonzalvo Maletra,* ordered that the two ships be unloaded and left part of their crew on land, captured the rest, and then burned the ships. On one of these ships, he found a Jewess *The Jewess* from Seville who said she had fled on account of the In- *from Seville* quisition from Spain to Barbary and then to Alexandria in Egypt and from there to Cairo and India. She said that at the time of the disagreement between our ships and the King of Calicut she was on land and she had heard that the King had been the cause of the discord, for he had allowed himself to be persuaded by other merchants that our people were thieves and were going to destroy his country. This Jewess, whom the Captain did not want to leave on land, a few days later threw herself into the sea and drowned. Because of this information, it was then deemed opportune to proceed, and having arrived above Calicut at *Arrival at* the mouth of the harbor, they fired all the artillery, which *Calicut* sank three ships of those which were in the harbor, and then got ready to leave. And not very far away, they captured a ship of the King of Calicut, from which they have brought to me some jewels of great price, 1500 pearls, amounting to 8000 ducats, three astrological instruments of silver, not in use amongst our astrologers. They are large and well made, and have been extremely useful to me. They say that the King of Calicut had sent the afore-mentioned ship to an island called Saponin † to obtain these instruments and to get a good pilot and a navigation chart for those lands. Now the pilot is in our hands, and I am having our language taught to him since he shows an understanding of these astrological instruments. The rest of the crew of this ship, together with the ship itself, were burned be-

* Barros (*op. cit.*, 66) identifies the Captain of this fleet as João da Nova.
† Saponin was located at the southern end of the Maldive Islands by Johann Ruysch on his 1508 world map.

fore the harbor of Calicut. When the King learned this, he went to Pandarani, a seaport, and ordered that some ships be armed in order to overcome our four ships which for 20 days had never left the coast of Calicut, doing as much damage as possible. Sighting the armada, our Captain went to meet it, having confidence in the fact that the ships of the Moors do not sail against the wind. And so the 15th of December of that year, in the afternoon, at about 16 miles south of this side of Calicut, they met and caught that armada to leeward, the wind being light. At the first encounter they sank two ships, since these were, as I have written above, weak and built with canes, and then the artillery and fire destroyed and burned three others. Since night was falling, the battle was ended. And let us thank God that none of our people died, although some of them were badly wounded; and this was caused by the fact that they never attempted to board the ships of their enemies as the latter were trying to do. The following morning, not sighting the mentioned armada anywhere, they moved toward Calicut and in the harbor they found this armada put in a state of defense. After having besieged it for five continuous days, and since the armada did not want to leave the harbor and fight, the Captain decided to go back to Lisbon, as he did not believe that anyone should land. This in spite of the fact that the King of Cananor, who was friendly to us, had asked through messages that our Captain land, but the Captain was never informed of this.*

War against the armada of Calicut

Five Moorish ships are lost

Our armada returns to Lisbon

And so, on the 20th of January 1502, they set sail for our lands. Rounding the Cape of Good Hope, one of the ships got lost in a storm. We still have no news of this ship; we believe it was lost. Later on, with a prosperous wind, the other three ships arrived in our harbor, on the 11th of September of that year, laden with those spices, drugs, jewels,

* Presumably the messages did not reach him.

14

and pearls which they had taken from the three ships previously captured. Before I received news from these two ships, fearing that they had been lost, I sent that same year, 1502 on the 3rd of March, another armada to those lands, made up of 25 ships, 12 ours and 13 belonging to merchants, the smallest being of 200 short tons. The Captain of this armada was Pedro Álvares Cabral,* who had also been the Captain of the first armada. And I ordered that six of these ships should go to the mouth of the Red Sea in order that no ship whatever be allowed to come out. The other ships were to go to Calicut and, without condition of peace, do as much damage as possible and then load either at Cochin or at Cananor, as might seem best to the Captain; in due time he was to send back ten of these ships, loaded. The rest were ordered to remain to carry on the war against Calicut.

1502: twenty-five ships go to India

Upon their departure, they took along those two hostages of Cochin and that messenger of Cananor who had come with the first armada. These hostages went away very happy and very willing to go back. All these ships arrived where they had been sent. Those six ships arrived at the mouth of the Red Sea; Captain Rodrigo Pallares is in charge of them. I shall advise your Majesty of these ships later on. The others first went to the King of Cananor, to whom the Captain had sent letters with his own messengers. They were well treated by him, and friendship was reaffirmed. The Captain took some goods because he wished to go to Calicut and to Cochin. And thus, with 19 ships, he passed by Calicut where for many days he did inestimable damage by land and by sea. And although conditions of peace had been offered to him by the King he refused them. Afterwards, the Captain went to the King of Cochin and, hav-

Six ships go to the Red Sea

* According to Barros (*op. cit.*, 70) Cabral had been considered for the command, but because of his dissatisfaction with limitations placed upon his authority the command was given to Vasco da Gama.

ing been graciously received, sent to land the two hostages whom he held and, thanks to them, he landed along with the hostages and found my factor and the seven Christians who had remained and had been well treated. And he gave to the said King our letters and the gifts listed herewith, for the good way he had treated our first armada: a crown of gold with enamel and jewels, a nightshade of gold worked with crescent-shaped rings, two large silver pitchers for a sideboard, well worked, two large and fine carpets, two satin cloths with figures, a field pavilion with all the furnishings, well worked, a cloth of carmine silk and one of taffeta. These were greatly welcome by the King, especially when he saw the pavilion set up out of doors. There they signed peace and friendship and the King granted a house to our factor with permission to trade as fully as he wishes. Beside this, he sent to me letters and the following listed gifts: two gold bracelets with many jewels according to their customs, a silver candelabrum ten palms high, well worked, two pieces of very sheer white cotton cloth, a stone as large as a cobnut. He wrote to me that this stone came from the head of a very rare animal, called burgoldaf, and it protects one against any kind of poison. And so there they loaded seven ships with spices and drugs and they also bought some jewels. We sent two Italian jewelers, who came from Rome, with this armada and he wanted them to remain there to buy jewels in our name; but they fled, as soon as they were landed, to the King of Calicut. According to what we have heard, they are using their knowledge to cast artillery. From there the armada departed, leaving the factor and certain other Christians. Going by Calicut to the shore, they took some prisoners, among which there were two of those Christians who had remained on land wounded at the time of the first armada. They are now with us. These two Christians, together with those who

Gifts to the King of Cochin

Stone against poisoning

16

had remained at Cochin, have told us of the customs and manners of their country, since they have lived there all this time in the houses of Moors. This armada arrived at Cananor where, in peace and friendship, they loaded three other ships. And thus ten ships, having arrived laden, left for Lisbon the 28th of December of that year 1502. And on their way back one of them got lost. We have heard that it got lost by the coast of the land of Santa Cruz. The others arrived to safety on the 1st of September 1503 with many spices. If God wills it, we intend to send a ship with these spices by the coast of Spain and another by the coast of Italy up to Venice, so that it may be known that both our armadas and our expenses are not thrown to the wind. All our other ships remain there according to their orders. The customs and manners of Calicut and of India, as we have learned through the two ransomed Christians and those of Cochin, are these: Calicut is a city on the continent, the main business center of India. Its latitude is 5°. It is large and not enclosed by walls, with sparse houses built of marble and lime, covered by palms with woods carved with some of their images. The people are not very black. They have gardens abundant with every fruit, with fountains where they bathe, since everyone is compelled to bathe himself three times a day. The King and gentlemen whom they call "chaffer" are idolaters. These go naked from the waist up, and cover themselves below the waist with a cloth of cotton and always have an unsheathed sword and a buckler. The swords are wider at the point than in any other place; the bucklers are round and very light, of many colors. All these are gentlemen; their ears are perforated with hanging jewels. They are married to more than one woman and because of this they do not care about their chastity. The women similarly go naked as the men, with their beautiful hair disheveled. The vir-

Three ships are loaded

Arrival in Lisbon

Customs of India

17

gins, just as soon as they can, indulge their lust because otherwise they would not be able to procure a husband. Almost anyone who takes a wife first asks that one of his prelates appointed for this should sleep with her. They hold it a fault to stain themselves with the blood

of one whom they love. The women eat no more than twice a day and eat rice, milk, butter, sugar, fruit, and drink water and nothing else. Before eating, they wash themselves. If perchance they should be touched by anyone who has not washed himself, they have to wash themselves again; and in this matter they are most ceremonious. Anyone who can eats every morning an herb called betel, which makes the lips red and the teeth black. They abstain from this herb for some time when they are melancholy. The King has two wives, each one attended by some priests, who, during the King's absence, sleep with them. On this account the children of the King do not succeed him, but only his nephews, sons of his brothers. An infinite number of women live in the King's house who sweep and wash wherever the King goes. They wash with very fine and embroidered cloths. The King has himself

carried on a litter which they call "andor," carried by men. Musicians of various kinds walk around it. However, no one can ever come nearer to him than three fathoms because he cannot be touched except by certain appointed people. Anyone speaking to him must hold his head lowered and his hands before his mouth. They pay their respects by joining their hands above their head. Artisans and men of low rank, such as fishermen, may not speak to him. The King, the gentlemen, and the women, when they die, are burned. The King is burned with sandalwood; the other people of low rank are buried, their shoulders and their head covered with ashes. They go shaved and with their beard and hair combed. Their lips are long and large and they believe in enchantments. They write on palm leaves with a steel stylus without ink. The merchants called "guzerats," of Cambay, who live in Calicut, are idolaters just like those of Calicut, so much so that among them whoever kills a cow is killed for it. They do not eat anything that can die nor do they drink wine. And if anyone eats meat by mistake, even though still a child, he is deprived of his lineage. They are whiter than the natives of Calicut. They wear beards and long hair combed in the manner of women. They are very chaste and a man has one woman and no more. They are merchants of cloths of linen and cotton, and jewelry. There are other Negroes called Gentiles, very lustful idolaters, merchants of jewels, pearls, gold, and silver, very much given to enchantment in such a fashion that they say that they are able to speak with the spirits at their will. There are many Moors of Mecca, Turkey, Babylonia, Persia, and other parts and therefore there is trade of all goods, like jewels, pearls, pestles, moss, amber, benzoin, incense, aloe wood, porcelain, rhubarb, cloves, cinnamon, sandals, lace, nutmegs, mace, ginger, pepper, tamarinds, myrobalan, and cassia fistula, and most other goods. We shall write in other letters about their countries of origin, their measures, and prices. There they use gold Venetian ducats and gold coins, as well as silver and metal coins. They call a silver coin *fanone*; 20 of these are equal to a ducat. The *tare* is another metal coin; 15 of these equal a *fanone*. The ships usually leave from Calicut in the month of November for Mecca, laden with spices. These spices go to Cairo and to Alexandria by land, where they are loaded for Venice. Further inland there is another kingdom of idolaters, bordering on Calicut, called Barsingua, which is abundant with horses and elephants experienced in warfare. In this kingdom women are burned in the sepulcher of their husbands. In the year 1503 we did not send any ship on a voyage because we were waiting for news from the 25 ships sent the preceding year. And when the news arrived in the month of September there was not sufficient time to send any ship until the following year, 1504. As to how we sent them we shall inform Your Majesty below.

Six loaded ships return to Lisbon

This did not prevent the Captain of the 25 ships who was in India from sending me in the year 1504 six ships laden with spices which arrived on the 28th of August of the same year. Two of these ships were from those which were at the strait of the Red Sea; the other four were from those of the armada of the Captain. Through these four ships we heard how all that time our Captain had been at war with the King of Calicut, whose losses and disgrace were so great that no ship dared going to Calicut; and that the afore-mentioned King more than once had sent messengers to the man demanding an agreement, but the Captain had not wanted to hear of it. This time they burned 21 ships

Twenty-one Moorish ships are burned

above the port of Calicut and from these he got many spices and drugs which he loaded on the six ships. Besides, he sent me six vases of porcelain, very excellent and large; six silver pitchers with certain other vases of their fashion for a sideboard; an ornament of their idols, of gold, two palms long with many fine stones, among which there is a very fine carbuncle of the value of a golden ducat, or a little more; an image of one of their idols, a thing quite deformed, made of gold and weighing about 30 pounds. In place of the eyes, it has two fine and well-set emeralds. The four ships of the armada have brought these things. The two ships which have been at the strait of the Red Sea relate that all those parts are frightened and that no ship has ever gone out from the strait nor entered it. Although twice the armada of the Sultan came to capture them, it has always returned, having lost some ship; in such a way by this time they have burned 16 large ships. At their depart-

20

ure, they learned that the Sultan was preparing a large armada in which there were many Christians, bombardiers, and much artillery and slender galleys; with God's will in brief time we shall take care of them. From the burned ships, they have brought to me, among other things, about 500 pounds of small pearls and about 40 pounds of pearls, each one of high price; eight shells with their own pearl inside, two of which I send to your Most Serene Majesty, so that you will be able to see their quantity and quality; a pear-shaped diamond, large as a good-sized bean, and some other jewels; two large lions as domesticated as dogs, with two Moors who take care of them; two Persian horses, one a starred bay, the other grey, not very large but very handsome and better racers than any other horse I have ever seen; and other animals unknown in our lands. Furthermore, since they have journeyed all over the coast from Malindi to Calicut, they have told us the following particularities of that shore. First there is the kingdom of Madagascar, a large and beautiful city, with much cavalry and not too mercantile. Further on there is an island, called Zanzibar, populated, with a bridge of a mile and one-half which connects it with the continent. Then there is the strait of the Red Sea which is six miles wide, where our ships have never entered. On the other side there is the Persian Sea where there is a small island called Jullfar, abundant with jewels of every kind. At the mouth of this sea there is another island called Ormuz where there are abundant pearls of all kinds, and horses which all throughout those lands are in great esteem. These two islands belong to a Moorish King. Then there is Cambay, which belongs to a big and mighty King, a very fertile land with every known product: wax, sugar, incense, silk and cotton cloths, horses, and many elephants. This king was an idolater, but a few years ago he was converted to the Mohammedan re-

The city of Madagascar

Island of Zanzibar

ligion. It is a city of many goods, as it borders with Arabia and India. By that coast they go to Calicut, where there are many other kingdoms and cities, as it is shown on the navigation map. These ships had not yet returned when I had already sent, in the month of February, 12 ships of which Loppo Soarez was the Captain. And now they have returned. When they left from here I gave them letters to be delivered to the King of Malindi, friendly to us, together with the following things: a saddle, a headpiece, a pair of stirrups, spurs, a breast harness for horses, made of silver, enameled with braids of gold and carmine; a bed canopy of gilded carmine silk, with four cushions, two of brocade and two of crimson velvet; a large fine carpet; a cloth of satin with figures; two pieces of scarlet and one of carmine silk to make one of their garments, which they call "merlota," and a piece of crimson taffeta to line this garment. This present was graciously received by the king, who came down to the shore. His priests sacrificed a ram over which he passed. He was accompanied by many people with many bowls of perfumes and he asked the Captain to remain in his harbor for nine days, ordering that provisions of all sorts, with the exception of bread which they do not have, be provided to all our people without any payment whatever. And he witnessed the demonstration of furnishings for a horse, something which I had sent, which pleased him greatly since they do not use such things. He sent me back two musical instruments with the masters who play them, one called Qualtref, the other Mischatot, very pleasant to hear; and he also sent me some jewels and very sheer linen cloths. Hence the armada left for Calicut, and joining with the other, they received a message from the King of Calicut; and the Captain parleyed with him about a pact—as he had advised him. Each one of them was seated in a barge on the sea. And first my Captain demanded that the two jewelers who had fled from the preceding armada be given back along with a knight called Rodrigo Rainell whom the King had retained, breaking the agreement. The King wanted to discuss other matters first. And so they disagreed and they departed from each other. The armada went to Cochin and part of it went beyond to Qualin where there are many Christians who have many spices. And while they were loading, they learned that in Calicut there were 15 large ships which were loading spices. Having received this news, they left for Calicut where they found these ships ready and laden with people; for this reason they pretended to be on their way. At night they turned around and the next morning were upon them. Since they had not been warned, they were captured. Having led them out of the harbor, they unloaded and burned them, and then sailed toward our land. On the 2nd of this month the 12 *Fifteen ships* ships I sent arrived laden with spices. The others are still there. By God's will, the following year we sent two ships laden with spices toward the East, in order that we would not be accused, as in the case of the ship belonging to our merchant Bartolomeo Fiorentino, of sailing across by way of Provence. With this ship, there arrived two other ships. The Captain of one is Ruy Lorenzo; Saldagna is the Captain of the other. As in the past year, they left from here with an armada to go to those lands, and luckily they succeeded in entering the Red Sea, in the islands of which they remained for 16 months. Our other armada has received news from them. During this time, they captured many ships and burned them, and have made many raids on land, since one of these ships is a *tafforea*, which carries 20 horses *The* tafforea and has its poop open with a bridge 30 fathoms long which *ship* is thrown on land. By means of this bridge, the horses can land and return aboard. In this fashion, they have done great damage, so much indeed that a King of Canibar and

23

the King of Barbary, mighty lords, donated them 30,000 gold *mitricale* in order to be left in peace; a *mitricale* is equivalent to one and one-half ducats in our monetary system. These ships have brought this money and many other riches. In the present year, during the month of March, we sent to those lands 30 well-armed ships which have been ordered to send back those ships which are part of the armada. Two of these ships have been ordered to discover the island of Sumatra * which is said to be nearby. Four of these ships must go to Sofala, where it is hoped trading will be allowed. We shall wait for what is to happen and we will prepare other ships for next year. May God preserve your most Serene Majesty for a long time in a tranquil way, and may He preserve us together with you, so that we might see our navigation both peaceful and successful to the greater glory and increase of Our Holy Faith.

Printed in Rome by Master Joanni di Besicken in 1505 the 23rd of October.

---

* *The Voyage of Pedro Álvares Cabral to Brazil and India*, transl. with introduction and notes by William Brooks Greenlee (London: The Hakluyt Society, 1938), p. 113, notes the confusion in the location of Ceylon and Sumatra at this time.

This book, in Linotype Janson on Corinthian text, was designed by Jane McCarthy of the University of Minnesota Press. It was printed at the Lund Press of Minneapolis, and bound at the A. J. Dahl Company of Minneapolis. Of the limited edition of 1000 copies, this is copy number

543

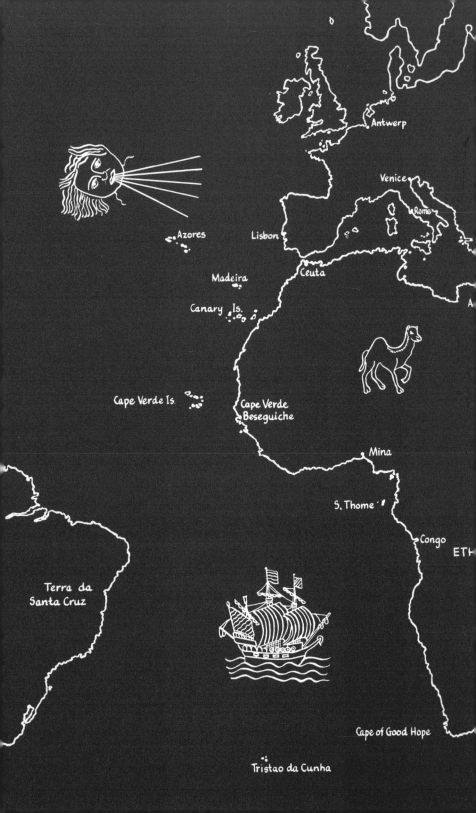

Antwerp

Venice

Rome

Azores

Lisbon

Madeira

Ceuta

Canary Is.

Cape Verde Is.

Cape Verde
Beseguiche

Mina

S. Thome

Congo

ETH

Terra da
Santa Cruz

Cape of Good Hope

Tristao da Cunha